Cooking with Chocolate: 50 Decadent Recipes

By: Kelly Johnson

Table of Contents

- Classic Chocolate Lava Cake
- Chocolate-Dipped Strawberries
- Chocolate Mousse
- Chocolate Truffles
- Chocolate Fondue
- Flourless Chocolate Cake
- Chocolate-Covered Pretzels
- Chocolate Fudge Brownies
- Dark Chocolate Almond Bark
- Triple Chocolate Cheesecake
- Chocolate Soufflé
- Hot Chocolate with Whipped Cream
- Chocolate Chip Cookies
- Chocolate-Peanut Butter Cups
- Chocolate-Covered Marshmallows
- Chocolate-Pistachio Cake
- Chocolate Eclairs
- Chocolate Panna Cotta
- Chocolate Ganache Tarts
- Chocolate-Coconut Macaroons
- White Chocolate Raspberry Cheesecake
- Chocolate Banana Bread
- Chocolate-Dipped Biscotti
- Chocolate-Coffee Mousse
- Mocha Chocolate Cupcakes
- Chocolate Coconut Truffles
- Chocolate Caramel Tart
- Chocolate-Covered Cherries
- Chocolate-Coffee Brownies
- Chocolate-Crunch Bars
- Chocolate Hazelnut Spread
- Chocolate Silk Pie
- Chocolate-Dipped Waffle Cones
- Dark Chocolate Raspberry Bark
- Chocolate-Covered Oreo Cookies

- Chocolate Almond Croissants
- Chocolate-Coconut Cupcakes
- Chocolate Soufflé for Two
- Chocolate-Covered Espresso Beans
- Chocolate-Coconut Energy Balls
- Chocolate Pudding
- White Chocolate Macadamia Nut Cookies
- Chocolate-Dipped Biscotti
- Chocolate Mint Cheesecake
- Chocolate-Covered Peanut Butter Balls
- Chocolate Peanut Butter Fudge
- Chocolate-Dipped Fruit Skewers
- Chocolate Raspberry Trifles
- Chocolate Buttermilk Cake
- Chocolate-Covered Popcorn

Classic Chocolate Lava Cake

Ingredients:

- 1/2 cup unsalted butter
- 6 oz bittersweet chocolate, chopped
- 1/2 cup powdered sugar
- 2 large eggs
- 2 large egg yolks
- 1 teaspoon vanilla extract
- 1/4 cup all-purpose flour
- Pinch of salt
- Butter and flour for greasing ramekins
- Optional: ice cream or whipped cream for serving

Instructions:

1. Preheat the oven to 425°F (220°C). Grease four 6-ounce ramekins with butter and dust with flour.
2. In a microwave-safe bowl, melt the butter and chocolate together, stirring until smooth. Let it cool slightly.
3. In a separate bowl, whisk together the eggs, egg yolks, powdered sugar, and vanilla extract until light and frothy.
4. Gently fold the melted chocolate mixture into the egg mixture, then sift in the flour and salt. Mix until combined.
5. Divide the batter evenly among the ramekins.
6. Bake for 12–14 minutes, or until the edges are set but the center is still soft.
7. Let the cakes sit for 1 minute, then invert onto plates. Serve warm with a scoop of ice cream or whipped cream.

Chocolate-Dipped Strawberries

Ingredients:

- 1 lb fresh strawberries, washed and dried
- 8 oz semisweet or dark chocolate, chopped
- 1 tablespoon coconut oil (optional for smoothness)
- White or milk chocolate (optional, for drizzling)

Instructions:

1. Line a baking sheet with parchment paper.
2. Melt the dark chocolate and coconut oil (if using) in a heatproof bowl over simmering water or in the microwave in 30-second intervals, stirring until smooth.
3. Hold each strawberry by the stem and dip it into the melted chocolate, covering about two-thirds of the berry.
4. Place the dipped strawberries on the prepared baking sheet and let them cool for 10–15 minutes.
5. Optional: Melt white or milk chocolate and drizzle over the dipped strawberries for decoration.
6. Serve once the chocolate has set.

Chocolate Mousse

Ingredients:

- 6 oz semisweet or bittersweet chocolate, chopped
- 3 large eggs, separated
- 1/4 cup heavy cream
- 1 tablespoon sugar
- 1/2 teaspoon vanilla extract
- Pinch of salt

Instructions:

1. Melt the chocolate over a double boiler or in the microwave, then let it cool slightly.
2. In a separate bowl, whip the heavy cream until soft peaks form. Set aside.
3. In another bowl, beat the egg yolks with sugar and vanilla extract until light and fluffy.
4. Fold the melted chocolate into the egg yolk mixture.
5. In a clean bowl, beat the egg whites with a pinch of salt until stiff peaks form. Gently fold the egg whites into the chocolate mixture.
6. Fold in the whipped cream.
7. Spoon the mousse into serving cups and chill for at least 2 hours before serving.

Chocolate Truffles

Ingredients:

- 8 oz semisweet or dark chocolate, chopped
- 1/2 cup heavy cream
- 1 teaspoon vanilla extract
- Cocoa powder, chopped nuts, or sprinkles for coating

Instructions:

1. Heat the heavy cream in a saucepan over medium heat until it begins to simmer. Remove from heat.
2. Pour the hot cream over the chopped chocolate and let it sit for 1-2 minutes. Stir until smooth.
3. Stir in the vanilla extract.
4. Refrigerate the chocolate mixture for 1-2 hours, or until firm enough to scoop.
5. Once chilled, use a spoon to scoop the mixture and roll it into balls.
6. Coat the truffles in cocoa powder, chopped nuts, or sprinkles.
7. Store in the fridge until ready to serve.

Chocolate Fondue

Ingredients:

- 8 oz semisweet or dark chocolate, chopped
- 1/2 cup heavy cream
- 1 tablespoon brandy or vanilla extract (optional)
- Fruit, marshmallows, and pound cake for dipping

Instructions:

1. Heat the heavy cream in a saucepan over medium heat until it begins to simmer.
2. Remove from heat and stir in the chopped chocolate until smooth.
3. Add brandy or vanilla extract if desired.
4. Transfer the chocolate mixture to a fondue pot, and keep warm over low heat.
5. Serve with dippable items like fruit, marshmallows, and cake cubes.

Flourless Chocolate Cake

Ingredients:

- 1 cup semisweet chocolate chips
- 1/2 cup unsalted butter
- 3/4 cup granulated sugar
- 1/4 teaspoon salt
- 1/4 cup cocoa powder
- 3 large eggs
- 1 teaspoon vanilla extract

Instructions:

1. Preheat the oven to 375°F (190°C). Grease and line an 8-inch round cake pan with parchment paper.
2. Melt the butter and chocolate together in a saucepan or microwave.
3. Stir in the sugar, salt, and cocoa powder.
4. Add the eggs, one at a time, beating well after each addition. Stir in the vanilla extract.
5. Pour the batter into the prepared pan and bake for 20–25 minutes.
6. Let the cake cool in the pan for 10 minutes, then turn out onto a wire rack to cool completely.
7. Serve as is or dust with powdered sugar.

Chocolate-Covered Pretzels

Ingredients:

- 1 bag of mini pretzels
- 8 oz semisweet or milk chocolate, chopped
- 1 tablespoon coconut oil (optional)

Instructions:

1. Line a baking sheet with parchment paper.
2. Melt the chocolate and coconut oil (if using) over a double boiler or in the microwave, stirring until smooth.
3. Dip each pretzel halfway into the melted chocolate and place it on the baking sheet.
4. Refrigerate the pretzels for 10–15 minutes, or until the chocolate sets.

Chocolate Fudge Brownies

Ingredients:

- 1 cup unsalted butter
- 1 cup granulated sugar
- 1/2 cup brown sugar
- 4 large eggs
- 1 teaspoon vanilla extract
- 1 cup all-purpose flour
- 1/2 cup cocoa powder
- 1/2 teaspoon salt
- 1 cup semisweet chocolate chips

Instructions:

1. Preheat the oven to 350°F (175°C). Grease a 9x9-inch baking pan.
2. Melt the butter in a saucepan over low heat.
3. Stir in the granulated sugar, brown sugar, eggs, and vanilla extract until smooth.
4. Sift the flour, cocoa powder, and salt together and fold into the wet ingredients.
5. Stir in the chocolate chips.
6. Pour the batter into the prepared pan and bake for 25-30 minutes, or until a toothpick comes out with a few moist crumbs.
7. Let the brownies cool before slicing.

Dark Chocolate Almond Bark

Ingredients:

- 8 oz dark chocolate, chopped
- 1/2 cup roasted almonds, chopped
- 1/4 teaspoon sea salt (optional)

Instructions:

1. Line a baking sheet with parchment paper.
2. Melt the dark chocolate over a double boiler or in the microwave.
3. Stir in the chopped almonds and mix well.
4. Pour the chocolate mixture onto the prepared baking sheet and spread into an even layer.
5. Sprinkle with sea salt if desired.
6. Refrigerate for 30 minutes, or until the bark hardens.
7. Break into pieces and serve.

Triple Chocolate Cheesecake

Ingredients:

- **For the crust:**
    - 1 1/2 cups chocolate cookie crumbs
    - 1/4 cup granulated sugar
    - 1/4 cup unsalted butter, melted
- **For the cheesecake filling:**
    - 3 (8 oz) packages cream cheese, softened
    - 1 cup granulated sugar
    - 3 large eggs
    - 1 cup sour cream
    - 1/2 cup heavy cream
    - 6 oz semisweet chocolate, melted
    - 6 oz white chocolate, melted
    - 1/2 teaspoon vanilla extract
- **For the topping:**
    - 3 oz milk chocolate, melted
    - Chocolate shavings (optional)

Instructions:

1. Preheat the oven to 325°F (165°C). Grease a 9-inch springform pan and line the bottom with parchment paper.
2. For the crust, mix the cookie crumbs, sugar, and melted butter in a bowl. Press the mixture into the bottom of the prepared pan. Bake for 10 minutes, then set aside to cool.
3. For the filling, beat the cream cheese and sugar until smooth and creamy. Add eggs one at a time, beating well after each addition. Stir in sour cream, heavy cream, melted semisweet chocolate, white chocolate, and vanilla extract.
4. Pour the filling over the crust and smooth the top. Bake for 55-60 minutes, or until the center is set but still slightly jiggly. Turn off the oven and let the cheesecake cool in the oven with the door slightly ajar for 1 hour.
5. Once cooled, refrigerate for at least 4 hours or overnight.
6. Before serving, drizzle with melted milk chocolate and garnish with chocolate shavings, if desired.

Chocolate Soufflé

Ingredients:

- 1/2 cup unsalted butter
- 1/2 cup all-purpose flour
- 1 1/4 cups milk
- 1/2 cup granulated sugar
- 1/4 teaspoon salt
- 1 teaspoon vanilla extract
- 6 oz semisweet chocolate, chopped
- 4 large eggs, separated
- 1/4 teaspoon cream of tartar

Instructions:

1. Preheat the oven to 375°F (190°C). Grease four 6-ounce ramekins and dust with cocoa powder.
2. In a saucepan, melt the butter over medium heat. Stir in the flour and cook for 1 minute. Gradually add the milk, whisking constantly until the mixture thickens. Stir in the sugar, salt, and vanilla extract.
3. Remove from heat and add the chopped chocolate, stirring until melted and smooth. Let the mixture cool slightly.
4. In a separate bowl, beat the egg yolks until light and fluffy. Stir them into the chocolate mixture.
5. In another bowl, beat the egg whites and cream of tartar until stiff peaks form. Gently fold the beaten egg whites into the chocolate mixture.
6. Spoon the batter into the prepared ramekins, filling them almost to the top. Bake for 12-15 minutes, or until puffed and set. Serve immediately.

Hot Chocolate with Whipped Cream

Ingredients:

- 2 cups whole milk
- 1/2 cup heavy cream
- 4 oz semisweet chocolate, chopped
- 2 tablespoons sugar
- 1/2 teaspoon vanilla extract
- Whipped cream (for topping)

Instructions:

1. In a medium saucepan, heat the milk and heavy cream over medium heat until hot but not boiling.
2. Add the chopped chocolate and sugar, stirring until the chocolate is fully melted and the mixture is smooth.
3. Remove from heat and stir in the vanilla extract.
4. Pour the hot chocolate into mugs and top with whipped cream. Serve immediately.

Chocolate Chip Cookies

Ingredients:

- 2 1/4 cups all-purpose flour
- 1/2 teaspoon baking soda
- 1/2 teaspoon salt
- 1 cup unsalted butter, softened
- 3/4 cup granulated sugar
- 3/4 cup packed brown sugar
- 1 teaspoon vanilla extract
- 2 large eggs
- 2 cups semisweet chocolate chips

Instructions:

1. Preheat the oven to 375°F (190°C) and line baking sheets with parchment paper.
2. In a medium bowl, whisk together the flour, baking soda, and salt.
3. In a large bowl, cream together the butter, granulated sugar, and brown sugar until light and fluffy. Beat in the vanilla extract and eggs, one at a time.
4. Gradually add the dry ingredients to the wet ingredients, mixing until just combined. Stir in the chocolate chips.
5. Drop spoonfuls of dough onto the prepared baking sheets, spacing them 2 inches apart.
6. Bake for 8-10 minutes, or until the edges are golden brown. Let cool on the baking sheet for a few minutes before transferring to a wire rack.

Chocolate-Peanut Butter Cups

Ingredients:

- 1 1/2 cups semisweet chocolate chips
- 1/2 cup creamy peanut butter
- 1 tablespoon unsalted butter
- 1 cup powdered sugar
- 1/2 teaspoon vanilla extract

Instructions:

1. Line a muffin tin with cupcake liners.
2. Melt the chocolate chips and butter together in a microwave or double boiler, stirring until smooth.
3. Spoon a small amount of melted chocolate into each cupcake liner, just enough to cover the bottom. Place the tin in the freezer for 10 minutes to set.
4. In a bowl, mix together the peanut butter, powdered sugar, and vanilla extract until smooth.
5. Spoon a dollop of peanut butter mixture onto each chocolate layer. Then, top with the remaining melted chocolate, covering the peanut butter completely.
6. Refrigerate for 30 minutes, or until set. Serve chilled.

Chocolate-Covered Marshmallows

Ingredients:

- 1 cup semisweet chocolate chips
- 1 tablespoon vegetable oil
- 10-12 large marshmallows
- Sprinkles or crushed nuts (optional)

Instructions:

1. Line a baking sheet with parchment paper.
2. Melt the chocolate chips and vegetable oil in a microwave or double boiler, stirring until smooth.
3. Insert a toothpick or skewer into each marshmallow and dip it into the melted chocolate, coating it completely.
4. Place the chocolate-covered marshmallows on the prepared baking sheet. Sprinkle with optional toppings, such as sprinkles or crushed nuts.
5. Refrigerate for 15-20 minutes, or until the chocolate is set.

Chocolate-Pistachio Cake

Ingredients:

- 1 cup all-purpose flour
- 1/2 cup unsweetened cocoa powder
- 1 teaspoon baking powder
- 1/2 teaspoon salt
- 1/2 cup unsalted butter, softened
- 1 cup granulated sugar
- 2 large eggs
- 1/2 teaspoon vanilla extract
- 1/2 cup buttermilk
- 1/2 cup pistachios, chopped
- 1/2 cup semisweet chocolate chips

Instructions:

1. Preheat the oven to 350°F (175°C) and grease a 9-inch round cake pan.
2. In a medium bowl, whisk together the flour, cocoa powder, baking powder, and salt.
3. In a large bowl, cream together the butter and sugar until light and fluffy. Beat in the eggs and vanilla extract.
4. Gradually add the dry ingredients to the wet ingredients, alternating with the buttermilk. Mix until just combined.
5. Stir in the chopped pistachios and chocolate chips.
6. Pour the batter into the prepared cake pan and smooth the top.
7. Bake for 25-30 minutes, or until a toothpick comes out clean. Let cool completely before serving.

Chocolate Eclairs

Ingredients:

- **For the choux pastry:**
    - 1 cup water
    - 1/2 cup unsalted butter
    - 1 cup all-purpose flour
    - 1/4 teaspoon salt
    - 4 large eggs
- **For the filling:**
    - 2 cups heavy cream
    - 1/4 cup powdered sugar
    - 1 teaspoon vanilla extract
- **For the glaze:**
    - 4 oz semisweet chocolate, chopped
    - 2 tablespoons heavy cream

Instructions:

1. Preheat the oven to 400°F (200°C) and line a baking sheet with parchment paper.
2. In a saucepan, bring the water and butter to a boil. Stir in the flour and salt, and cook for 1-2 minutes until the mixture forms a dough.
3. Remove from heat and beat in the eggs one at a time, mixing until smooth.
4. Spoon the dough into a piping bag and pipe 3-inch long eclairs onto the prepared baking sheet.
5. Bake for 20-25 minutes, or until golden brown. Let cool completely.
6. For the filling, beat the heavy cream, powdered sugar, and vanilla extract until stiff peaks form. Fill the eclairs with whipped cream using a piping bag.
7. For the glaze, melt the chocolate and heavy cream together until smooth. Drizzle over the filled eclairs.
8. Serve immediately or refrigerate until ready to enjoy.

Chocolate Panna Cotta

Ingredients:

- 1 1/2 cups heavy cream
- 1/2 cup whole milk
- 1/2 cup granulated sugar
- 8 oz semisweet chocolate, chopped
- 1 teaspoon vanilla extract
- 1 packet unflavored gelatin (about 1 tablespoon)
- 2 tablespoons water

Instructions:

1. In a saucepan, combine the heavy cream, milk, and sugar. Heat over medium heat until the sugar dissolves and the mixture begins to simmer.
2. Remove from heat and stir in the chopped chocolate until melted and smooth.
3. In a small bowl, sprinkle the gelatin over the water and let it sit for 5 minutes to bloom. Then, stir it into the warm chocolate mixture until dissolved.
4. Stir in the vanilla extract.
5. Pour the mixture into individual ramekins or serving glasses and refrigerate for at least 4 hours or until set.
6. Serve chilled, optionally topped with whipped cream or fresh berries.

Chocolate Ganache Tarts

Ingredients:

- **For the crust:**
    - 1 1/2 cups chocolate cookie crumbs
    - 1/4 cup granulated sugar
    - 1/2 cup unsalted butter, melted
- **For the ganache:**
    - 8 oz semisweet chocolate, chopped
    - 1/2 cup heavy cream
    - 2 tablespoons unsalted butter

Instructions:

1. Preheat the oven to 350°F (175°C). Grease and line tart pans with removable bottoms.
2. Combine the chocolate cookie crumbs, sugar, and melted butter. Press into the bottom of the tart pans to form an even crust.
3. Bake the crusts for 8-10 minutes, then remove and cool completely.
4. For the ganache, heat the heavy cream in a saucepan over medium heat until it begins to simmer. Pour it over the chopped chocolate and let it sit for 2-3 minutes. Stir until smooth.
5. Stir in the butter until fully combined.
6. Pour the ganache into the cooled tart crusts and smooth the tops.
7. Refrigerate for at least 2 hours, or until the ganache is set.
8. Serve chilled, optionally topped with whipped cream or fresh fruit.

Chocolate-Coconut Macaroons

Ingredients:

- 2 1/2 cups shredded unsweetened coconut
- 1/2 cup semisweet chocolate chips
- 1/4 cup granulated sugar
- 2 large egg whites
- 1 teaspoon vanilla extract
- Pinch of salt

Instructions:

1. Preheat the oven to 350°F (175°C). Line a baking sheet with parchment paper.
2. In a bowl, mix together the coconut, sugar, and salt.
3. In a separate bowl, beat the egg whites until soft peaks form.
4. Fold the egg whites into the coconut mixture, then stir in the vanilla extract.
5. Scoop spoonfuls of the mixture onto the prepared baking sheet, forming mounds.
6. Bake for 12-15 minutes, or until the macaroons are golden brown.
7. Melt the chocolate chips in a microwave or double boiler, then drizzle over the cooled macaroons.
8. Let the chocolate set before serving.

White Chocolate Raspberry Cheesecake

Ingredients:

- **For the crust:**
    - 1 1/2 cups graham cracker crumbs
    - 1/4 cup sugar
    - 1/2 cup unsalted butter, melted
- **For the cheesecake filling:**
    - 16 oz cream cheese, softened
    - 1/2 cup white chocolate chips, melted
    - 1 cup sour cream
    - 3/4 cup granulated sugar
    - 3 large eggs
    - 1 teaspoon vanilla extract
    - 1/2 cup fresh raspberries

Instructions:

1. Preheat the oven to 325°F (163°C). Grease and line a 9-inch springform pan.
2. For the crust, combine the graham cracker crumbs, sugar, and melted butter. Press the mixture into the bottom of the prepared pan and bake for 10 minutes.
3. For the filling, beat the cream cheese and sugar until smooth. Add the eggs one at a time, beating well after each addition.
4. Stir in the melted white chocolate and vanilla extract. Add the sour cream and mix until smooth.
5. Gently fold in the raspberries, being careful not to crush them.
6. Pour the mixture over the cooled crust and smooth the top.
7. Bake for 50–60 minutes, or until the cheesecake is set and slightly golden.
8. Let cool completely, then refrigerate for at least 4 hours before serving.

Chocolate Banana Bread

Ingredients:

- 2 ripe bananas, mashed
- 1 cup granulated sugar
- 2 large eggs
- 1/2 cup unsalted butter, melted
- 1 3/4 cups all-purpose flour
- 1/2 cup unsweetened cocoa powder
- 1 teaspoon baking soda
- 1/4 teaspoon salt
- 1/2 cup semisweet chocolate chips

Instructions:

1. Preheat the oven to 350°F (175°C). Grease a 9x5-inch loaf pan.
2. In a bowl, mix the mashed bananas, sugar, eggs, and melted butter until combined.
3. In another bowl, whisk together the flour, cocoa powder, baking soda, and salt.
4. Gradually add the dry ingredients to the wet ingredients, mixing until just combined. Fold in the chocolate chips.
5. Pour the batter into the prepared loaf pan and bake for 60-70 minutes, or until a toothpick comes out clean.
6. Let cool in the pan for 10 minutes before transferring to a wire rack to cool completely.

Chocolate-Dipped Biscotti

Ingredients:

- 2 cups all-purpose flour
- 1 cup granulated sugar
- 1 teaspoon baking powder
- 1/2 teaspoon salt
- 2 large eggs
- 1 teaspoon vanilla extract
- 1/2 cup chopped almonds
- 6 oz semisweet chocolate, chopped

Instructions:

1. Preheat the oven to 350°F (175°C). Line a baking sheet with parchment paper.
2. In a bowl, combine the flour, sugar, baking powder, and salt.
3. In a separate bowl, whisk the eggs and vanilla extract until combined.
4. Stir the wet ingredients into the dry ingredients, then fold in the almonds.
5. Shape the dough into a log and place it on the prepared baking sheet.
6. Bake for 25-30 minutes, or until golden brown. Let cool for 10 minutes, then slice into 1-inch pieces.
7. Arrange the slices on the baking sheet and bake for an additional 10-12 minutes, until crispy.
8. Melt the chocolate and dip the ends of the biscotti into the chocolate. Let the chocolate set before serving.

Chocolate-Coffee Mousse

Ingredients:

- 6 oz semisweet chocolate, chopped
- 1 cup heavy cream
- 2 tablespoons sugar
- 1 tablespoon instant coffee granules
- 2 large egg whites
- 1 tablespoon granulated sugar

Instructions:

1. Melt the chocolate in a heatproof bowl over a double boiler or in the microwave. Let cool slightly.
2. In a saucepan, heat the heavy cream, sugar, and coffee granules until simmering. Remove from heat and pour over the melted chocolate. Stir until smooth.
3. In a separate bowl, beat the egg whites with the sugar until stiff peaks form.
4. Gently fold the egg whites into the chocolate mixture until combined.
5. Spoon the mousse into serving glasses and refrigerate for at least 2 hours before serving.

Mocha Chocolate Cupcakes

Ingredients:

- 1 cup all-purpose flour
- 1/2 cup cocoa powder
- 1 teaspoon baking soda
- 1/2 teaspoon baking powder
- 1/4 teaspoon salt
- 1/2 cup granulated sugar
- 1/2 cup brown sugar, packed
- 1/2 cup unsalted butter, softened
- 2 large eggs
- 1 teaspoon vanilla extract
- 1/2 cup brewed coffee, cooled
- 1/2 cup whole milk
- 1/2 cup semisweet chocolate chips

Instructions:

1. Preheat the oven to 350°F (175°C). Line a muffin tin with paper liners.
2. In a bowl, whisk together the flour, cocoa powder, baking soda, baking powder, and salt.
3. In a separate bowl, cream the butter, granulated sugar, and brown sugar until light and fluffy. Add the eggs and vanilla extract and mix until combined.
4. Gradually add the dry ingredients, alternating with the coffee and milk, until just combined. Stir in the chocolate chips.
5. Divide the batter evenly among the cupcake liners and bake for 18-20 minutes, or until a toothpick comes out clean.
6. Let cool completely before frosting or serving.

Chocolate Coconut Truffles

Ingredients:

- 1 1/2 cups shredded unsweetened coconut
- 8 oz semisweet chocolate, chopped
- 1/2 cup sweetened condensed milk
- 1/2 teaspoon vanilla extract
- 1/2 cup semisweet chocolate chips (for coating)

Instructions:

1. Melt the chopped chocolate with sweetened condensed milk over low heat, stirring until smooth.
2. Remove from heat and stir in shredded coconut and vanilla extract.
3. Allow the mixture to cool for about 10 minutes, then roll into small balls.
4. Melt chocolate chips and dip each ball, coating fully.
5. Place truffles on parchment paper and refrigerate for at least 30 minutes before serving.

Chocolate Caramel Tart

Ingredients:

- **For the crust:**
    - 1 1/2 cups chocolate cookie crumbs
    - 1/4 cup sugar
    - 1/2 cup unsalted butter, melted
- **For the caramel filling:**
    - 1 cup heavy cream
    - 1 cup brown sugar
    - 1/4 cup unsalted butter
    - 1 teaspoon vanilla extract
    - 1/4 teaspoon salt
- **For the chocolate ganache:**
    - 6 oz semisweet chocolate, chopped
    - 1/2 cup heavy cream

Instructions:

1. Preheat the oven to 350°F (175°C) and grease a tart pan.
2. Mix cookie crumbs, sugar, and melted butter. Press into the tart pan and bake for 10-12 minutes. Let cool.
3. For the caramel, simmer heavy cream, brown sugar, butter, and salt until combined and smooth. Stir in vanilla extract.
4. Pour caramel over the cooled crust and chill for 1 hour.
5. For the ganache, heat cream and pour over chopped chocolate. Stir until smooth. Pour ganache over the caramel layer.
6. Chill tart for 2 hours before serving.

Chocolate-Covered Cherries

Ingredients:

- 16 oz maraschino cherries, drained and patted dry
- 8 oz semisweet chocolate, chopped
- 1/4 cup heavy cream

Instructions:

1. Insert a toothpick into each cherry and set aside.
2. Melt the chocolate with the cream over low heat, stirring until smooth.
3. Dip each cherry into the melted chocolate, covering it completely.
4. Place the cherries on parchment paper and refrigerate until the chocolate hardens.

Chocolate-Coffee Brownies

Ingredients:

- 1/2 cup unsalted butter
- 1 cup sugar
- 2 large eggs
- 1 teaspoon vanilla extract
- 1/2 cup all-purpose flour
- 1/4 cup cocoa powder
- 1/2 teaspoon baking powder
- 1/4 teaspoon salt
- 2 tablespoons instant coffee granules, dissolved in 2 tablespoons hot water
- 1/2 cup semisweet chocolate chips

Instructions:

1. Preheat the oven to 350°F (175°C). Grease and line a baking pan with parchment paper.
2. Melt butter and sugar in a saucepan, stirring until smooth. Remove from heat.
3. Add eggs and vanilla extract, whisking until combined.
4. Sift in flour, cocoa powder, baking powder, and salt. Add dissolved coffee and mix until smooth.
5. Stir in chocolate chips, then pour the batter into the pan.
6. Bake for 20-25 minutes or until a toothpick comes out clean. Let cool before slicing.

Chocolate-Crunch Bars

Ingredients:

- 3 cups rice cereal
- 2 cups semisweet chocolate chips
- 1/2 cup peanut butter
- 1 teaspoon vanilla extract

Instructions:

1. Melt chocolate chips and peanut butter in a saucepan over low heat, stirring until smooth.
2. Remove from heat and stir in vanilla extract.
3. Pour the rice cereal into a large bowl and pour the melted chocolate mixture over it. Stir gently to coat.
4. Press the mixture into a greased pan and refrigerate for 1 hour before cutting into bars.

Chocolate Hazelnut Spread

Ingredients:

- 1 1/2 cups roasted hazelnuts
- 1 cup semisweet chocolate, chopped
- 2 tablespoons cocoa powder
- 1/4 cup powdered sugar
- 1/4 teaspoon vanilla extract
- Pinch of salt
- 1/4 cup vegetable oil

Instructions:

1. In a food processor, blend roasted hazelnuts until smooth and creamy.
2. Melt the chocolate and add to the hazelnut paste along with cocoa powder, powdered sugar, vanilla extract, and salt. Blend until smooth.
3. Gradually add vegetable oil until the mixture reaches your desired consistency.
4. Transfer to a jar and refrigerate.

Chocolate Silk Pie

Ingredients:

- **For the crust:**
    - 1 1/2 cups chocolate cookie crumbs
    - 1/4 cup sugar
    - 1/2 cup unsalted butter, melted
- **For the filling:**
    - 1 1/2 cups semisweet chocolate chips
    - 1 1/2 cups heavy cream
    - 1 teaspoon vanilla extract
    - 3 large egg yolks
    - 1/4 cup sugar

Instructions:

1. Preheat oven to 350°F (175°C). Grease and line a pie dish.
2. Combine cookie crumbs, sugar, and melted butter. Press into the pie dish and bake for 10 minutes. Let cool.
3. For the filling, melt chocolate chips and cream together, stirring until smooth.
4. Whisk egg yolks with sugar, then slowly add the chocolate mixture, whisking continuously.
5. Pour into the cooled crust and bake for 20-25 minutes. Let cool, then chill for 2 hours before serving.

Chocolate-Dipped Waffle Cones

Ingredients:

- 4 waffle cones
- 8 oz semisweet chocolate, chopped
- 1/2 cup crushed nuts or sprinkles (optional)

Instructions:

1. Melt the chocolate in a heatproof bowl over simmering water.
2. Dip the tops of the waffle cones into the melted chocolate, then sprinkle with nuts or sprinkles, if desired.
3. Place the cones on parchment paper and refrigerate until the chocolate sets.

Dark Chocolate Raspberry Bark

Ingredients:

- 8 oz dark chocolate (70% cocoa or higher)
- 1/2 cup freeze-dried raspberries
- 1/4 cup slivered almonds (optional)

Instructions:

1. Melt the dark chocolate in a heatproof bowl over simmering water, stirring until smooth.
2. Line a baking sheet with parchment paper and pour the melted chocolate onto it, spreading evenly.
3. Sprinkle the freeze-dried raspberries and slivered almonds over the chocolate.
4. Refrigerate for 30 minutes or until set. Once hardened, break into pieces and enjoy.

Chocolate-Covered Oreo Cookies

Ingredients:

- 12 Oreo cookies
- 8 oz semisweet or milk chocolate, chopped
- Sprinkles or crushed nuts (optional)

Instructions:

1. Melt the chocolate in a microwave or using a double boiler, stirring until smooth.
2. Dip each Oreo into the melted chocolate, coating it completely.
3. Place the dipped cookies on parchment paper and sprinkle with sprinkles or crushed nuts if desired.
4. Refrigerate for 20-30 minutes until the chocolate sets.

Chocolate Almond Croissants

Ingredients:

- 1 sheet puff pastry, thawed
- 1/4 cup dark chocolate chips
- 1/4 cup sliced almonds
- 1 egg (for egg wash)
- 1 tablespoon sugar (for sprinkling)

Instructions:

1. Preheat oven to 375°F (190°C) and line a baking sheet with parchment paper.
2. Roll out the puff pastry sheet and cut into triangles.
3. Place a small amount of chocolate chips in the center of each triangle, and sprinkle with sliced almonds.
4. Roll up each triangle into a croissant shape and place on the baking sheet.
5. Brush with egg wash and sprinkle with sugar.
6. Bake for 15-20 minutes or until golden brown. Let cool before serving.

Chocolate-Coconut Cupcakes

Ingredients:

- **For the cupcakes:**
    - 1 1/2 cups all-purpose flour
    - 1/2 cup unsweetened cocoa powder
    - 1 teaspoon baking powder
    - 1/2 teaspoon baking soda
    - 1/2 teaspoon salt
    - 1/2 cup unsalted butter, softened
    - 1 cup sugar
    - 2 large eggs
    - 1 teaspoon vanilla extract
    - 1/2 cup coconut milk
    - 1/2 cup shredded coconut
- **For the frosting:**
    - 1/2 cup unsalted butter, softened
    - 1 1/2 cups powdered sugar
    - 2 tablespoons unsweetened cocoa powder
    - 1 tablespoon coconut milk
    - 1/2 cup shredded coconut (for topping)

Instructions:

1. Preheat the oven to 350°F (175°C) and line a muffin tin with cupcake liners.
2. In a bowl, whisk together flour, cocoa powder, baking powder, baking soda, and salt.
3. In another bowl, beat butter and sugar until fluffy. Add eggs one at a time, beating well after each addition.
4. Mix in vanilla extract, then alternate adding the dry ingredients and coconut milk until smooth. Stir in shredded coconut.
5. Divide the batter into cupcake liners and bake for 18-20 minutes, or until a toothpick comes out clean. Let cool.
6. For the frosting, beat butter, powdered sugar, cocoa powder, and coconut milk until smooth. Frost the cooled cupcakes and sprinkle with shredded coconut.

Chocolate Soufflé for Two

Ingredients:

- 2 oz semisweet chocolate, chopped
- 2 tablespoons unsalted butter
- 1/4 cup sugar
- 2 large eggs, separated
- 1/2 teaspoon vanilla extract
- Pinch of salt
- Powdered sugar (for dusting)

Instructions:

1. Preheat the oven to 375°F (190°C). Grease two ramekins and dust them with sugar.
2. Melt chocolate and butter in a heatproof bowl over simmering water, stirring until smooth.
3. In a separate bowl, beat egg yolks and sugar until light and fluffy. Stir in melted chocolate and vanilla extract.
4. In another bowl, beat egg whites and salt until stiff peaks form.
5. Gently fold the egg whites into the chocolate mixture, being careful not to deflate the air.
6. Divide the batter evenly between the ramekins and bake for 12-15 minutes or until puffed and set.
7. Dust with powdered sugar and serve immediately.

Chocolate-Covered Espresso Beans

Ingredients:

- 1 cup espresso beans
- 8 oz semisweet or dark chocolate, chopped
- 1/2 teaspoon vanilla extract

Instructions:

1. Melt the chocolate in a heatproof bowl over simmering water, stirring until smooth. Stir in vanilla extract.
2. Gently dip each espresso bean into the melted chocolate, coating it completely.
3. Place the coated beans on parchment paper to set. Refrigerate for 30 minutes or until the chocolate hardens.

Chocolate-Coconut Energy Balls

Ingredients:

- 1 cup rolled oats
- 1/2 cup shredded unsweetened coconut
- 1/4 cup dark chocolate chips
- 1/4 cup almond butter
- 2 tablespoons honey or maple syrup
- 1 teaspoon vanilla extract
- Pinch of salt

Instructions:

1. In a large bowl, combine oats, shredded coconut, chocolate chips, almond butter, honey, vanilla, and salt.
2. Stir until well mixed. Roll the mixture into small balls (about 1 inch in diameter).
3. Place the balls on a parchment-lined baking sheet and refrigerate for 30 minutes before serving.

Chocolate Pudding

Ingredients:

- 2 cups whole milk
- 1/2 cup sugar
- 1/4 cup cornstarch
- 1/4 teaspoon salt
- 4 large egg yolks
- 6 oz semisweet chocolate, chopped
- 1 teaspoon vanilla extract

Instructions:

1. In a medium saucepan, whisk together the milk, sugar, cornstarch, and salt. Bring to a simmer over medium heat, stirring constantly.
2. In a separate bowl, whisk the egg yolks. Slowly add a small amount of the hot milk mixture to the yolks, whisking constantly, to temper them.
3. Gradually whisk the egg yolk mixture into the saucepan with the remaining milk mixture. Cook over medium heat until thickened, about 5 minutes.
4. Remove from heat and stir in the chopped chocolate and vanilla extract until smooth.
5. Pour the pudding into serving cups and refrigerate for at least 2 hours before serving.

White Chocolate Macadamia Nut Cookies

Ingredients:

- 1 1/2 cups all-purpose flour
- 1/2 teaspoon baking soda
- 1/4 teaspoon salt
- 1/2 cup unsalted butter, softened
- 1/2 cup brown sugar, packed
- 1/4 cup granulated sugar
- 1 large egg
- 1 teaspoon vanilla extract
- 1 cup white chocolate chips
- 1 cup macadamia nuts, chopped

Instructions:

1. Preheat the oven to 350°F (175°C) and line a baking sheet with parchment paper.
2. In a medium bowl, whisk together the flour, baking soda, and salt.
3. In a large bowl, cream together the butter, brown sugar, and granulated sugar until light and fluffy.
4. Beat in the egg and vanilla extract.
5. Gradually add the dry ingredients to the wet ingredients, mixing until just combined.
6. Stir in the white chocolate chips and macadamia nuts.
7. Drop spoonfuls of dough onto the prepared baking sheet, spacing them about 2 inches apart.
8. Bake for 10-12 minutes or until the edges are golden brown. Let cool on the baking sheet for a few minutes before transferring to a wire rack.

Chocolate-Dipped Biscotti

Ingredients:

- 2 cups all-purpose flour
- 1 teaspoon baking powder
- 1/2 teaspoon salt
- 1/2 cup sugar
- 3 large eggs
- 1 teaspoon vanilla extract
- 1/2 cup chocolate chips (for dipping)
- 1/4 cup chopped pistachios or almonds (optional)

Instructions:

1. Preheat the oven to 350°F (175°C) and line a baking sheet with parchment paper.
2. In a medium bowl, whisk together the flour, baking powder, and salt.
3. In a separate bowl, beat together the sugar, eggs, and vanilla extract until smooth.
4. Gradually add the dry ingredients to the wet ingredients, mixing until combined.
5. Turn the dough onto a lightly floured surface and knead briefly. Shape the dough into a log and place it on the prepared baking sheet.
6. Bake for 25-30 minutes or until golden brown. Let the log cool for about 10 minutes before slicing it into 1/2-inch pieces.
7. Place the biscotti back on the baking sheet and bake for another 10-12 minutes, flipping them halfway through.
8. Once cooled, melt the chocolate chips and dip the biscotti in the melted chocolate. Let the chocolate set before serving.

Chocolate Mint Cheesecake

Ingredients:

- **For the crust:**
    - 1 1/2 cups chocolate cookie crumbs
    - 1/4 cup melted butter
    - 2 tablespoons sugar
- **For the cheesecake filling:**
    - 3 (8 oz) packages cream cheese, softened
    - 1 cup granulated sugar
    - 1 teaspoon vanilla extract
    - 3 large eggs
    - 1/2 cup sour cream
    - 1/4 cup heavy cream
    - 1/2 teaspoon mint extract
    - 1/2 cup chopped mint chocolate

Instructions:

1. Preheat the oven to 325°F (165°C). Grease a 9-inch springform pan.
2. Combine the cookie crumbs, melted butter, and sugar in a bowl. Press the mixture into the bottom of the prepared pan.
3. Beat the cream cheese and sugar in a large bowl until smooth. Add the eggs one at a time, beating well after each addition.
4. Stir in the sour cream, heavy cream, and mint extract. Fold in the chopped mint chocolate.
5. Pour the filling over the crust and smooth the top. Bake for 50-60 minutes, or until the edges are set and the center is slightly jiggly.
6. Let the cheesecake cool completely, then refrigerate for at least 4 hours before serving.

Chocolate-Covered Peanut Butter Balls

Ingredients:

- 1 cup peanut butter
- 2 cups powdered sugar
- 1 1/2 cups graham cracker crumbs
- 1/4 cup unsalted butter, melted
- 8 oz semisweet chocolate, chopped

Instructions:

1. In a medium bowl, mix the peanut butter, powdered sugar, graham cracker crumbs, and melted butter until smooth.
2. Roll the mixture into small balls, about 1 inch in diameter, and place them on a parchment-lined baking sheet.
3. Melt the chocolate in a microwave or double boiler, stirring until smooth.
4. Dip each peanut butter ball into the melted chocolate, coating it completely. Place it back on the parchment paper.
5. Refrigerate for 30 minutes until the chocolate sets.

Chocolate Peanut Butter Fudge

Ingredients:

- 1 cup creamy peanut butter
- 1 cup semisweet chocolate chips
- 1 can (14 oz) sweetened condensed milk
- 1/2 teaspoon vanilla extract
- 1/4 teaspoon salt

Instructions:

1. Line an 8-inch square baking pan with parchment paper.
2. In a medium saucepan, melt the peanut butter and chocolate chips over low heat, stirring until smooth.
3. Stir in the sweetened condensed milk, vanilla extract, and salt.
4. Pour the mixture into the prepared pan and spread evenly.
5. Refrigerate for at least 2 hours until set. Cut into squares and serve.

Chocolate-Dipped Fruit Skewers

Ingredients:

- 1 cup dark or milk chocolate chips
- 1 tablespoon coconut oil (optional, for smooth dipping)
- 1 cup strawberries, hulled
- 1 cup banana slices
- 1 cup pineapple chunks
- 1 cup apple slices

Instructions:

1. Melt the chocolate chips and coconut oil (if using) in a microwave or double boiler until smooth.
2. Thread the fruit onto wooden skewers, alternating between strawberries, bananas, pineapple, and apples.
3. Dip the fruit skewers into the melted chocolate, coating them halfway or completely, as desired.
4. Place the dipped skewers on a parchment-lined tray and refrigerate for 15-20 minutes until the chocolate sets.

Chocolate Raspberry Trifles

Ingredients:

- 1 box chocolate cake mix (or homemade chocolate cake)
- 1 pint fresh raspberries
- 2 cups whipped cream or whipped topping
- 1 cup chocolate ganache (made with equal parts cream and chocolate)
- 1/4 cup raspberry jam

Instructions:

1. Prepare the chocolate cake according to package instructions and allow it to cool completely.
2. Once cooled, crumble the cake into small pieces.
3. Layer the cake, whipped cream, raspberries, raspberry jam, and chocolate ganache in individual cups or a large trifle dish.
4. Repeat the layers until the dish is full, finishing with a layer of whipped cream and raspberries.
5. Refrigerate for at least 2 hours before serving.

Chocolate Buttermilk Cake

Ingredients:

- 1 1/2 cups all-purpose flour
- 1/2 cup unsweetened cocoa powder
- 1 teaspoon baking soda
- 1/4 teaspoon salt
- 1/2 cup unsalted butter, softened
- 1 cup sugar
- 2 large eggs
- 1 teaspoon vanilla extract
- 1 cup buttermilk
- 1/2 cup boiling water

Instructions:

1. Preheat the oven to 350°F (175°C) and grease two 8-inch round cake pans.
2. In a bowl, whisk together the flour, cocoa powder, baking soda, and salt.
3. In another bowl, cream together the butter and sugar until light and fluffy. Beat in the eggs and vanilla extract.
4. Alternate adding the dry ingredients and buttermilk to the butter mixture until smooth.
5. Stir in the boiling water to thin the batter.
6. Divide the batter evenly between the pans and bake for 30-35 minutes, or until a toothpick comes out clean.
7. Let the cakes cool completely before frosting.

Chocolate-Covered Popcorn

Ingredients:

- 1/2 cup unpopped popcorn kernels
- 1 cup semisweet chocolate chips
- 1 tablespoon vegetable oil
- 1/4 teaspoon sea salt

Instructions:

1. Pop the popcorn according to package instructions.
2. Melt the chocolate chips and vegetable oil together in a microwave or double boiler until smooth.
3. Pour the melted chocolate over the popcorn, stirring to coat evenly.
4. Spread the popcorn onto a parchment-lined baking sheet and sprinkle with sea salt.
5. Let the chocolate set at room temperature or refrigerate for faster results.